WHAT GOES AROUND
COMES AROUND

WHAT GOES AROUND COMES AROUND

Emmanuel Zirimwabagabo

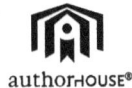

authorHOUSE®

AuthorHouse™ LLC
1663 Liberty Drive
Bloomington, IN 47403
www.authorhouse.com
Phone: 1-800-839-8640

Story by Emmanuel Episcopere Ziri
Telephone (Canada) 17807180989

Translated by Eden Translators International Director:
Linah Wakungi +254726838822

Published by AuthorHouse   09/21/2013

ISBN: 978-1-4918-1704-9 (sc)
ISBN: 978-1-4918-1703-2 (e)

Library of Congress Control Number: 2013917405

CONTENTS

Appreciation

This book is dedicated to you my dear mother Mwavita Mugereza and my dear sister Tantine Lubala Nabintu. You have been there for me during my tough times and your true love has been my strength everyday. May the Lord grant you long life full of blessings. I would like to thank Almighty God above all, He has been a very present help all the time, in Him I have my hope and destiny secure all the time.

INTRODUCTION

Emmanuel, at a young age attended a school in Uvira Congo. It was not until the civil war that broke in Congo and everything lost meaning for Emmanuel. His father was mercilessly butchered at the war, and in the midst of the whole confussion, his family fled to Canada while he was still in school one afternoon.

Emmanuel struggled alone. Fear and frustrations became the order of the day. For survival and for his own security he moved from one refugee camp to another. In 1996, he finally settled in Nyarugusu refugee camp in Tanzania.

In Tanzania, life was not easy either. A camp that had many refugees from Congo too, he had to learn how to survive and continue with his education. He made new friends and one of them was Rehema who was his classmate in the refugee camp. They both assisted each other in revising for all subjects. As they had a custom of revising together, one evening these two friends made love, though it was not Emmanuel's idea.

The following morning they went to school. They all sat for the test. Emmanuel passed the test but Rehema failed the test. When Rehema found out that she had failed the test she went to talk to her mathematics teacher.

SCENE ONE

Beginning of play

(Rehema and her mathematics teacher in staffroom)

TEACHER: How may I help you please?

REHEMA: I need your help please. I failed the mathematic's test that we did yesterday. This will make me not proceed with the next class.

TEACHER: (*laughing*) Oh . . . . yes. If you need any assistance, are you ready to give me what I ask from you?

REHEMA: Yes teacher. Whatever you ask I will give it to you.

TEACHER: Okay. Can I take you out this evening and spend time together with you?

REHEMA: Yes I am ready, if I will pass the test . . . .

(Rehema had sex with the teacher that evening, and afterwards the teacher made sure he changed her marks. After three months Rehema found out that she was pregnant.)

REHEMA: (*thinking and talking alone*) What will I do now? I am three months pregnant! I think it is better I see the teacher so that we can solve this.

Rehema goes to visit the teacher

TEACHER: Yes Rehema, tell me, how can I help you?

REHEMA: I went to see the doctor the other day and I found out that I was pregnant. You are responsible for my pregnancy! (*she talks as she shys away from the teacher. The teacher grabs her hand and takes her away to a more solitude place*)

TEACHER: Look here Rehema . . . I am a human being. I really helped you so please help me now too. I have an idea. We can work it out together.

REHEMA: What is your idea?

TEACHER: You are aware that as teachers we have a code of ethics that governs our conduct with the students that we teach? We are not supposed to get involved sexually with our students. If I am discovered, I can easily be jailed and how will you live alone? I promise to take care of your child if you cooperate with me. I don't want to loose my job. My family depends on me.

REHEMA: I did not come here for your lectures please!! Let me know your idea. I am suffering. Soon or later everybody will know I am pregnant! The other option I have is to go and tell the headmaster what you did to me!

TEACHER: Cool down Rehema. Please we can sort this out. I don't want to loosemy job. My idea is this,(*hesistantly*) I have watched you closely and have discovered that Emmanuel is your friend. I am sure you have been intimate friends. I will give you 15,000 US dollars, go and convince him that he is responsible for your pregnancy.

REHEMA: (*thinking*) I see. Your idea is not bad, but 15,000 US dollars is too little. May be 40,000 dollars can help me convince Emmanuel and in any case if he refuses, I can open a business to take care of myself.

TEACHER: Trully speaking, I don't have that amount, but I can get 20,000 US dollars.

REHEMA: I am not surprised that you want to give me 20,000 US dollars. What business do we have together in that we have to bargain what is rightful? What I am going through is really painful. My future dreams are all cut short because of this baby (*pointing at her stomach*). Listen to me very carefully, I have already given you a chance that you want to joke around with, you dont even care about my life all you care is about your reputation as a teacher.

TEACHER: Rehema please, lets not urgue about this. Please go see Emmanuel and if accepts the responsibility of the pregnancy then I will give you 40,000 US dollars. Time is not on our side.

REHEMA: Fine.

(*The teacher leaves as Rehema is left alone*)

REHEMA: If I approach Emmanuel and he refuses to take the responsibility, what will happen to me? I think it is better I tell teacher that Emmanuel has already

3

accepted the responsibity at least I will have the money at hand.

After two days . . . .

REHEMA: I have talked to Emmanuel and he has accepted to take the responsibility.

TEACHER: Thankyou very much Rehema! Here is the 40,000 dollars. Good luck!

REHEMA: It is now settled. Peace be with you. Goodbye.

They shake hands of agreement and Rehema leaves.

REHEMA: I have money now. The next thing I need to do is to look for Emmanuel so that I see if he can accept to take the responsibility.

Rehema goes to Emmanuel's house . . . .

REHEMA: Emmanuel, how have you been?

EMMANUEL: Long time Rehema! seems you have remembered me today. Where have you been since we did our exams in school?

REHEMA: It is a long story Emmanuel, but I am here now! Alot has happened since the last time I was with you and that is why I have decided to visit you today.

Emmanuel offers Rehema a seat and they all sit down. Rehema shys away from Emmanuel. She starts to talk hesitantly . . .

It is really a long time, since we made love together that night. I have missed my monthly periods and the other day I went to see a doctor, who confirmed that I am pregnant. That is the main reason I have come to see you today Emmanuel. I have no one to turn for help but you. I am now three months pregnant.

EMMANUEL: Rehema we only made love once. You mean out of that one day only you became pregnant? Is that possible really. *(he wakes up from his seat in shock and draws near to Rehema)*

REHEMA: Listen to me carefully, because you are educated. You know very well even three minutes are too many for conception to occur. All we need now is to agree on our next step.

EMMANUEL: Yes I know that very well, but also you know very well that I am student and I do abit of farm work. How shall we live?

REHEMA: Yes I know that very well, Emmanuel, we were all not xpecting this to happen, but for now we have no alternative since it has happened to me. Concerning how to live, it does not matter to me so much since we have lived in this camp and I cannot force you we change our lifestyle. If it is farming I know that very well. I a ready we do any work so that we can take care of our baby. We are all refugees.

EMMANUEL: I have no other choice but to accept the consequences and I cannot lure you to abortion, it is better we struggle at all cost. Welcome to my house Rehema. From today I take you as my wife.

Emmanuel holds her hand and does introduction of his house to her.

In the morning of the following day

EMMANUEL: Rehema, it is morning, let me go to the farm I look for yams. We have no food in the house for today.

REHEMA: Do you want us to go together?

EMMANUEL: No problem Rehema, we can go together.

At the farm . . . .

EMMANUEL: Rehema, you know very well that we only went to school together and we never got the chance to be so close in life like we are now. Since now we are living as couple, I think it is good you tell me more about you. What do you think?

REHEMA: Yes Emmanuel. That is very true. It is really a nice opportunity since we are now a couple and I have now to tell you everything about myself. In my family, we are five. My mother, one brother and two sisters. My mother told me that my father passed away long time ago because I never had the chance to see him and I am the last born in our family. My mother has managed to bring us up single handedly. After the war that broke up back in Congo, we moved to several refugee camps and finally we settled here in Nyarugusu camp. That is all about my family. What about your family?

EMMANUEL: I'm very sorry Rehema. My family is quite large. I have two sisters and four brothers, that makes us seven children and I am the fourth born in that family. I come from a poor background too. My father was a lawyer and he passed away in 1996 during the Congo civil war too. That makes the two of us! Since then, I am really grateful to God since my mother took the responsibility of taking good care of us. She oftenly reminded us that death was normal and despite of all that she gracefully managed to bring the seven of us up. Unfortunately, when the civil war broke out in the year 2002, I was still in school that evening that I will never forget. The teachers advised us to go home. When I arrived home, there was nobody. My entire family and all our neighbours had run away. I was stranded. I had no idea what to do. I had also to look for an alternative. I started a journey to nowhere that fateful evening. I found a group of people on the road, I followed them without knowing where to go. I did spend my life in several refugee camps, as we kept on being moved and eventually I found myself in this Nyarugusu camp here inTanzania. That is how I am here. I don't

	know where my family lives or if they were killed in the war.
REHEMA:	I am really sorry Emmanuel. Thanks be to God at least we are alive. It was such a fateful event.

After exchanging their life histories, that episode ends . . .

SCENE TWO

Life at the refugee camp

One day, after three months, Emmanuel wakes up to go to the farm as usual.

EMMANUEL: Good morning Rehema.

REHEMA: Good morning.

EMMAMUEL: I need to go the farm very early today to weed the maize before the sun becomes scotchingly hot.

REHEMA: It is alright Emmanuel. I am not feeling very well today. Have a nice day my dear.

EMMANUEL: It is alright. You will be well. The baby will be soon here.

As Emmanuel prepares to leave, someone knocks the door. Emmanuel goes to open the door.

EMMANUEL: Welcome.

PATRICK: Good morning.

EMMANUEL: Good morning.

PATRICK: My name is Patrick and I have been directed here as I am looking for a young man called Emmanuel.

EMMANUEL: You are in the right place. I am Emmanuel.

PATRICK: I don't live here, I come from Canada and I am here because I have a message for you Emmanuel. I need to make sure I am talking to the right person too.

EMMANUEL: My message? You come from Canada? Very well, have a seat please so that we can talk. This sounds very interesting. (*he offers him a seat*)

PATRICK: Thank you very much. As I have told you I am from Canada and I have a message for you from your mother. She has been looking for you in very many camps for several years. She gave me the job of doing that personally. It was not until few months ago, that we got the information that you live here in Nyarugusu camp in Tanzania. We communicated with the camp managers and we got your address and that is how I am here. It was not an easy task though.

EMMANUEL: Interesting . . . my mother . . . ? I almost forgot about my family since it has been years and I almost thought they were all killed in the war . . . . But . . . . wait a minute . . . . how do I prove that you are talking about my real mother?

PATRICK: He has told me that your name is Episcopere Lubala and people know you as Emmanuel . . . .

EMMANUEL: mmmmmm . . . .

PATRICK: I am not yet through . . . . your mother is called Mwavita Lubala and this is her photograph (*he gives him a photograph*)

EMMANUEL: (*he jumps up with joy*) I am satisfied Patrick as I know that is very true. It is true, she is the one, she still looks very beautiful.

PATRICK: I am very sorry for all the hardship you went through all those years but today you are comforted and it will be a nice day for you. Every cloud has a silver lining. Today is your day young boy.

EMMANUEL: (*In a reflective manner*) I have learned to endure a lot as this life has alot of challenges. One can struggle but not get, but the most important thing is not to give up. Challenges are part of life, they are unavoidable since it is part of life's journey and not any embarassment. But today, I can testify that the Lord is faithful in the land of the living.

PATRICK: Emmanuel, I have heard you and your struggles have come to an end. Your mother has given me money to give you and she also wants to talk to you over the phone. Hold on I give her a call . . . . (*he calls*) Yes . . . . I am fine . . . . Yes . . . . He is right here . . . . very well . . . . Hold on, I hand over the phone to emmanuel . . .

EMMANUEL: Hallo . . .

EMMANUEL'S MOTHER: Hallo, my son . . . .

EMMANUEL: Yes mum, I can't believe it. Your voice has never changed! I am very happy mum. Patrick has just told me that you are in Canada . . . .

EMMANUEL'S MOTHER: Yes my son, we are in Canada all of us ecxept you. I have been searching for you everywhere, but finally I got your address.

EMMANUEL: Thank you mum. How is the rest of the family?

EMMANUEL'S MOTHER: The rest of the family is fine . . . .

EMMANUEL: Okay mum. Pass my greetings to them all.

EMMANUEL'S MOTHER: Patrick will give you my number then we shall talk later . . .

EMMANUEL: Pass my greetings to all white people there too mum . . . (*excited*)

PATRICK: I hope you have heard it for yourself Emmanuel. Your mother has given me 300 US dollars to give it to you so that you can buy a mobile phone. You will be able to communicate with her any time. Here is also her number. I have to leave now since I have other commitments for the day.

EMMANUEL: Wait a minute . . . . how many dollars . . . . ?

PATRICK: 300 US dollars. Have a nice day. Good bye

Emmanuel bids goodbye to Patrick and he is left counting the money excitedly e and then afterwords he rushes back to tell his wife what has just ensued . . .

EMMANUEL: Rehema!! Rehema!! Wake up . . . .

REHEMA: What is wrong Emmanuel? Are you okay?

EMMANUEL: I can't believe my eyes Rehema . . . God is awesome!

REHEMA: Please, what is it Emmanuel? (*Rehema talks impatiently*)

EMMANUEL: I hope you remember what I shared with you about my family around three months ago . . . .

REHEMA: Yes . . . . and . . . .

EMMANUEL: In the morning, As I was just leaving the house to the farm, a visitor knocked the door, I opened the

	door for him, he introduced himself as Patrick from Canada . . .
REHEMA:	Mmmmm . . . from Canada? . . . . is he your friend . . . . ? What did he want from you such early in the morning . . . ?
EMMANUEL:	Hold on, the story is very interesting . . . Patrick is not my friend but he has brought very great news, that he has been send by my mother and she wanted to talk to me too. I hesitated because conmen are several here in the camp. I asked him several questions and he has been able to answer all, as a proof that trully he was talking of the right infomation. I have also talked to my mother on his mobile phone. Her voice has never changed! She also informed me that the rest of the family is with her in Canada and they are all fine.
REHEMA:	That is wonderful! I am so happy for you dear!(*Rehema draws near to Emmanuel and lowers her voice*) Have you also informed your mother that you have a wife too?
EMMANUEL:	Yes, I have.
REHEMA:	Mmmmm . . . Trully a good day is seen in the morning . . . Thank you God.
EMMANUEL:	Yes, and Patrick has also given me 300 US dollars from my mother. She has said I buy a phone today so that we can communicate any time. Patrick has also given me her number.
REHEMA:	Mmmm, I see . . . I don't think you are going to the farm any more?

EMMANUEL: You are very right. Don't you think it is a nice day for us to celebrate my love? I have just spoken to people from Canada . . . . We have dollars here now . . . Today we are going to celebrate and no going to the farm . . .

REHEMA: Mmm . . . the farm for the white people . . . . (*Rehema talks happily as she hugs Emmanuel*)

EMMANUEL: I will go to the market. I will buy meat at least for today . . . We have been feeding on vegetables . . .

REHEMA: (*She laughs loudly and happily*) Okay I get you. Please bring for me some oranges . . .

EMMANUEL: Okay, let me go to the market. See you later . . .

Emmanuel goes to the market and comes back later in the evening . . . .

EMMANUEL: Rehema . . . . Im back home . . . .

REHEMA: What have you bought for us?

EMMANUEL: I have bought a goat, today we shall have minced meat and I have also bought a mobile phone for us. Look, here it is. (*Rehema unpacks the phone and admires everything about it*)

REHEMA: This is wonderful. You are really wise. I am such a lucky woman to have a man like you.

EMMANUEL: I appreciate that my dear. Let me slaughter the goat so that you start cooking.

After a while the food is ready. They are sitted at the table eating . . .

REHEMA: My husband let's eat. God is great.

EMMANUEL: Mmmm . . . okay. Since we started living together you have never called me . . . my husband . . . today must be a great day!!

REHEMA: Not really Emmanuel. One secret of a woman is that when she really cooks good food she feels nice and feels even better to serve for her husband and that is why I have called you my husband . . . .

EMMANUEL: I must also congratulate you. You have cooked really nice food.

REHEMA: Thankyou. I do appreciate too.

EMMANUEL: I have also noticed that the meat is too much. What do you think . . . . we give a share to our neighbours?

REHEMA: I have also thought the same. Let's give them a share.

EMMANUEL: Okay, that will be fine. Let us then give to Kabongo's mother . . . . Kabibi's mother and chabusuki's mother.

REHEMA: Kabibi's mother . . . . how comes you are forgetting Kabwana's mother? (*smilling wittingly*)

EMMANUEL: Hah! You see how you women think? I have just said kabibi's mother and now you have said Kabwana's mother. I can see you are getting jealous now . . . .

REHEMA: Mmmm . . . that was just joke my love! You said today was a special day.

SCENE THREE

Emmanuel helps the less fortunate

After few days emmanuel goes on with his farm work. While Emmanuel was going to the farm he meets two children, Jack and Diume . . . .

EMMANUEL: Hey kids, what are you doing here? You are the ones who spoil my crops. Come here!

DIUME: We are not the ones who spoil your crops Sir. We are orphans and we are looking for work or any place, where can stay. We are hungry too. Please help us. (*they both kneel before him*)

EMMANUEL: I am very sorry. Please stand up. Are you brothers?

JACK: No, we are not brothers, but we have become like brothers due to hardship as we search for survival means. (*they stand up*)

DIUME: Please help us Sir . . .

EMMANUEL: What do you really need mostly kids . . . ? Food or a place to stay?

JACK: If you can give us a place to stay, we have alot that we can help you with. We can work for you everyday Sir. In the farm or in your house.

EMMANUEL: Okay. Let us go to my house . . .

They all go together as they talk. Eventualy they arrive home and Emmanuel welcomes them.

EMMANUEL:	Rehema . . . . Rehema . . . .
REHEMA:	Yes . . . .
EMMANUEL:	We have visitors here. These kids are orphans, I have met them on my way to the farm. They have no place to stay . . . I will invite them they introduce themselves to us. From today they will be staying with us. I would like you to prepare for them the extra room we have so that they can be sleeping there.
REHEMA:	Before you invite this kids here first, I think you have made a wrong decision. Anything can happen to these kids. They look very tired and very weak. What will you do if they die? (*Rehema talks softly to Emmanuel so that the kids don't listen to their conversation.*)
EMMANUEL:	Mmmm . . . . I think you are a selfish woman! I chose to assist the one who had good health. That is a selfish talk . . . Listen carefully, this is my house . . . I will do what is noble and what I think it is the best. Get off my way . . . . you have a very selfish heart.

This is my house, I will do what is noble (*He calls both of them loudly*) Diume and Jack, welcome . . . Feel free and stop crying. This is now your home henceforth. This is also your aunt, she is called Rehema.

They all settle and he makes them comfortable. End of that episode.

One morning, Jack, Diume and Emmanuel are playing cards.

JACK: I would like to ask you a question Emmanuel, if you don't mind. How do you live your life?

EMMANUEL: Good question Jack. I go to the farm almost everyday, then when I come I rest here. I rarely go to socialise with friends. It is also good that you have asked me that question, since I wanted to inform both of you that today I will be leaving for three months.

DIUME: Where are you going to? Please don't leave us behind.

EMMANUEL: Don't worry at all. As I had told you, I do farmwork. We ussually assist one another outside the province as farmers. I will be leaving, so I ask of you to please assist your aunt with any work and don't mind what she said when you came to this house. I will be back as soon as we are done.

JACK: Don't worry Emmanuel. We have lived such a hard life and we can cope with any situation. We wish you a safe journey. May God bless you. You are such a nice man.

EMMANUEL: Thank you.

Emmanuel leaves and the two boys are left with Rehema.

After two months Rehema delivers her baby.
In Emmanuel's house.

REHEMA: Jack and Diume . . . .

DIUME: Yes aunt . . .

REHEMA: I just gave birth yesterday night . . . .

DIUME: Congratulation aunt. We are here to help you please. Let me bring you food aunt . . . .

JACK: That is good news! Diume, please deal with the food as I go to collect firewood.

DIUME: That is very fine Jack.

Jack and Diume takes care of Rehema very well.

DIUME: Welcome back Jack. Seems you went to collect firewood in a nearby place.

JACK: I have done that so fast so that I can come back immediately and assist you as I knew you will have alot of work in the kitchen.

DIUME: Thank you very much, your food is in the kitchen.

REHEMA: Jack and Diume, could you please assist me with the house during this period?

JACK: No problem. We are here as your children, we must assist you.

After one month jack falls sick

REHEMA: How comes Diume you are working alone?

DIUME: Jack is sick . . . .

REHEMA: I think Jack is very lazy!

DIUME: Infact Jack works more often than me. He is very sick aunt . . . .

REHEMA:	Where is Jack?
DIUME:	He is resting aunt.
REHEMA:	Come here Diume . . . .
DIUME:	Yes.
REHEMA:	Even if he is sick, does he have to spit all over? Look at this . . .
DIUME:	Aunt, Jack is sick. That is why he is spitting.
REHEMA:	So because he is sick that is why he wants to spread the disease to everyone? What is wrong with you kids?

In the morning, the following day

DIUME:	Aunt, I am off to the river to fetch water.
REHEMA:	Okay Diume.

Rehema takes the opportunity to disturb Jack as Diume is away . . . .

REHEMA:	Wake up. Go look for firewood. Lazy boy . . . .
JACK:	Aunt, the firewood for yesterday is still there. Moreover, I am unwell . . .
REHEMA:	I see we are now urguing. Wake up very fast you go to the farm. Who do you think you are?
JACK:	I am unwell aunt. Have mercy on me.
REHEMA:	(*she throws cold water to Jack*) Wake up!!
JACK:	I am really feeling cold, then you throw cold water on me? Okay, let me go although I am in pain.

Jack leaves and Diume comes in.

REHEMA:	Welcome back Diume. You must be tired.
DIUME:	Yes during this summer season, it is really hard to get water. How is Jack fairing?
REHEMA:	I have send him to the farm.
DIUME:	oh no . . . aunt, you know very well Jack is unwell then you send him to the farm. You have a cruel heart.
REHEMA:	Who do you think you are to talk to me that way? Who is that that I can't send? I am in charge here.
DIUME:	I have not said that you can't send me though Jack is unwell . . .

Jack emerges with a load of firewood, but very sick

JACK:	Please off load me . . . .
DIUME:	Okay. Let me do it. How did you accept to go to the farm when you are sick?
JACK:	Diume, without wisdom, it is very hard to live with people. Aunt came to wake me up, thinking that she was bringing me medicine, she threw water on me. Just look at the bed it is very wet.
DIEUME:	I am very sorry. You will be alright Jack . . .

As Jack and Diume talks, Emmanuel emerges. They all rush to him and welcomes him happily.

DIUME:	Welcome back . . . .

EMMANUEL:	Thank you very much. Let me rest outside here. Jack bring me some water. I am very thirsty. How have you been?
DIUME:	We all fine. God has blessed aunt, she has given birth, although Jack is unwell.
EMMANUEL:	That is good news for the baby! Oh no . . . That is why he is not happy. You will be fine Jack. since I am back. Prepare yourself I take you to the dispensary. Where is your aunt?
JACK:	She is inside.

Emmanuel gets concerned with Jack's health. They all talk and after a while that episode ends there.

After two months . . . .

EMMANUEL:	Diume and Jack, come here . . . .
DIUME:	Yes . . .
EMMANUEL:	Let us go for a walk. I need to talk to both of you.

They all leave the house and Emmanuel talks to them

JACK:	I am really grateful that you came back. I feel better now.
EMMANUEL:	Jack I am very happy that you are healthy and strong now. I really love both of you and I would not wish

	you to struggle in this life. While I was away, how did you cope with your aunt Rehema?
JACK:	That is a very good question. She has a problem of not understanding people. If it were no for Diume, I almost gave up. She really gave me a hard time, I almost died.
EMMANUEL:	My young brothers, there something I had not told you about your aunt. We were going to the same school, we used to play together. All over sudden I impregnated her without my knowledge. This circumstance forced us to live together as a couple so that I could take care of her. Listen to me carefully, she is not my choice. She is a selfish woman. We only live together for convinience of the baby. My family lives in Canada, and she too well knows that. Only she does not know that I plan to go to Canada because if she discovers she can even kill me because we don't share the same blood. That is how I live with her. Women are not our family members and they can be very bad. That is all I wanted to tell you.
DIUME:	You really love us!! You even trust us with your deep secrets.
EMMANUEL:	Don't worry, life is about being there fo each other.
JACK:	what do you mean by that?
EMMANUEL:	I know both of you are still young. All I mean is that we are not realtives but we are there for each other.
JACK:	I know understand . . . .

EMMANUEL: Thank you for you company. I will always be there for
              you.

They talk a lot about their lives as Emmanuel encourages them.
All this time Emmanuel has also been communicating with his mother
and Patrick

After some few days, Patrick comes back to pick Emmanuel.

PATRICK: (*he knocks*)
EMMANUEL: Welcome back again Patrick . . .
PATRICK: Thank you very much. Most of the time, back in
              Canada we don't give notice of coming back . . . I am
              grateful.
EMMANUEL: I appreciate that. How is my mum back in Canada?
PATRICK: All of them are fine. Your mother has send me to take
              you to Canada in two days time.
EMMANUEL: You mean we are going to Canada together?
PATRICK: Yes, but I will give you two days of preparing yourself
              as I also try to prepare your travel documents.
EMMANUEL: Okay. That will be good. I will be ready in two days
              time.
PATRICK: Okay. See you in two days time.
EMMANUEL: Thank you. You are welcomed in my house any time.

Patrick leaves, Emmanuel wakes Jack and Diume

EMMANUEL: Jack and Diume, wake up . . .

JACK:	Emmanuel, you have woken up too early today. What is the matter?
EMMANUEL:	Jack, life gives no rest to a troubled man.
DIUME:	Any problem Emmanuel?
EMMANUEL:	All things are fine. I have just received very good news this morning from Patrick. I have always advised you not to give up. My mother wants me in Canada in two days time. I am telling you this because I will be leaving without telling your aunt Rehema.
DIEUME:	oh . . . . no . . . . Emmanuel you are leaving us. Anyway, we wish you all the best in life.
JACK:	The bible clearly states that there is enough grace for every temptation that we pass through in life. What a joy would be for you. in Canada. You will forget all struggles that you have endured here.
EMMANUEL:	I am so grateful for both of you. I believe it will be a safe journey. Please don't forget my advise because good days are ahead. I wouch will always keep in touch with both of you. Before I leave I will give you my mobile phone so that we can be communicating through it.

SCENE FOUR

Emmanuel's destiny with Canada

After two days, Patrick and Emmanuel leaves for canada.

Rachel (Emmanuel's sister) and Emmanuel's mother are at the Edmonton International Airport waiting for Emmanuels arrival.

RACHEL: Really it has been a long time since 1996 to 2012. I don't know if we can recognise him mum.

EMMANUEL'S MOTHER: No parent can forget their child. I see them. There they are together with Patrick!!

RACHEL: Welcome to Canada my brother Emmanuel!!!!!

(They all run towards them. Soft music is played from background as jubilation is seen as they exchange hugs and they leave for home.)

At the dining table, early in the morning the following day.

EMMANUEL'S MOTHER: Your sister was saying that I will not recognise you because it has been really a long time.

EMMANUEL: Ah! mum you had to recognise me!

RACHEL: Blood is thicker than water. I just saw you and said, there is my brother!

EMMANUEL: Oh sister you look so beautiful. Same to mum here.

RACHEL: You will still look better and more handsome. Canada food and lifestyle will change everything.

EMMANUEL'S MOTHER: Okay. Let's prepare we go show your brother around the city.

EMMANUEL: I am so excited. I can't believe my eyes I am in canada!

After a while the leave the house. Soft music plays on the background as they sight see the city. They take their time as they explain everything to Emmanuel.

EMMANUEL'S MOTHER: Oh my children let's go home. We cannot see everything in one day.

EMMANUEL: I am very happy to see such a wonderful world. I am grateful mum.

Next day . . .

RACHEL: Food is ready brother . . .

EMMANUEL: Im coming sister. Canada is really clean. I had a wonderful sleep.

RACHEL: It is 1200 hrs right now. You have slept according to African time.

EMMANUEL: How comes mum has not yet eaten?

EMMANUEL'S MOTHER: I am coming my son.

RACHEL: Just eat. Here we eat any time.

EMMANUEL'S MOTHER: That's true my son. Here we eat any time. Just eat. By the way, I need to know, what do you feel about your wife back in Africa?

EMMANUEL: That is a good question mother. I feel that it was an accident. She is free to get married to any other man and I am free to marry the woman of my choice. I will keep in communication with her through the two boys I was living with for the sake of my child. I left my mobile phone to the two boys.

RACHEL: Oh brother, many men are getting married from Africa. Why are you making such a decision?

EMMANUEL: Getting married in Africa is not a solution to marriage. Every marriage needs patience and respect. I had all that but my wife lacked that. I strongly feel she is not the best for me and further more from the beginning she was not my choice.

RACHEL: I understand brother. Here in Canada it is simple to get a girlfriend but it is very hard to get a wife.

EMMANUEL'S MOTHER: My children, I needed to know this so that I know if we could invite her here in Canada.

EMMANUEL: Oh that is good mother and also very kind of you. I came here without even saying goodbye to her. I really do not want her in my life but I will take the responsibility of the child.

RACHEL: I think that is very fine mother. I believe this will be sorted out with time. Let me take Emmanuel out for shopping.

EMMANUEL'S MOTHER: Okay. That is good. Please remember to buy for a calling card, so that Emmanuel can talk to Rehema back in Africa today in the evening.

RACHEL: Yes mum.

Soft music is played in background as they go to shopping malls. They go from one shopping mall to another at the same time Emmanuel is also learning a lot about Canada.

RACHEL: I think we have done enough shopping brother. Let's go and have a snack.

EMMANUEL: That's very okay. I am already feeling hungry.

Rachel takes Emmanuel to a buffet place.

RACHEL: Make sure you eat to the full brother.

EMMANUEL: Yes sister.

RACHEL: Feel free to eat anything you like.

EMMANUEL: Yes sister. Although I have noticed that there are no African dishes . . . .

RACHEL: Oh brother. African dishes people eat to fill up their tummies but here people eat what they desire. Make sure you take small portions of each.

EMMANUEL: Yes, think you are right. I have already gone for three rounds but if it were Ugali it would just be once.

Next day . . .

RACHEL: What do you think about going to salon brother?
EMMANUEL: Oh. I would really appreciate. I only felt shy to tell you about it.

RACHEL: Please be bold to tell me anything brother. Let us now go to salon then.

EMMANUEL: Okay.

Soft music from the background as they proceed to salon

EMMANUEL: Thank you Rachel. I feel great.

RACHEL: Okay we shall take some photographs later for
              facebook and you can send others back home in
              Africa to your friends.

EMMANUEL: What is facebook sister?

RACHEL: Facebook is a social media world. Through facebook
              you will get all friends and relatives. I mean you
              can get a wife or a husband. I don't mean another
              worldout of space but just a world over the internet.
              I am sure in out of 100% of people on earth 70 % are
              on facebook.

EMMANUEL: Oh, I see you are on facebook. Let me see if I can
              change my clothes so that I can have better pictures. I
              might get a wife! *(they all laugh)*

RACHEL: Okay do that. In facebook there are also angels!

*Rachel has been able to communicate to a photographer called James. As
they arrive home, the photographer comes in too.*

RACHEL: I see the photographer has just arrived. *(she opens the
              door)* Welcome James. How have you been?

JAMES: I am fine Rachel, thanks. Are you ready? I have another
              client in the next street so I need not stay for long.

RACHEL: Alright James. I had called to take my brother photographs. (she calls Emmanuel) Brother! Come the photographer is here with us.

EMMANUEL: Okay. Im coming right away.

They take many photographs in different positions and styles

EMMANUEL: Waoo!! Such nice photographs. Is this really me? He is an expert.

JAMES: Thank you. I am yet to edit them. They will be better than they appear.

RACHEL: James, when do we get the photographs?

JAMES: Today in the evening, they will be ready.

RACHEL: We are grateful James. We shall wait in the evening then.

JAMES: Okay, see you then later. (*he leaves the house*)

RACHEL: Okay let me assist you brother to open a facebook account. (*They sit down as Rachel opens her smart phone to teach Emmanuel*) What name would you prefer to use?

EMMANUEL: Use Episcopere Emmanuel.

RACHEL: Episcopere Emmanuel. Wow! what is the meaning of Episcopere? Nice name brother!

EMMANUEL: It means biscuits body . . . .

Rachel demonstrates using her phone the procedure on how to open an account stage by stage.

RACHEL: I have now opened your account brother. Biscuits body . . . . brother you are funny!! (*they all laugh happily*)

EMMANUEL: I am grateful sister. I have one more question. How does one use facebook? What next now sister?

RACHEL: Well, I don't get you well, what do you mean?

EMMANUEL: I mean, now I have a facebook account. I need to start communicating and utilising it. How do I do that and I don't have a computer or a internet connected phone?

RACHEL: Don't worry brother. I will give you mine and then I will buy another one. There you go . . . .

EMMANUEL: Okay sister. I hope to get the best of the best from facebook.

SCENE FIVE

Emmanuel meets his fiancee

Emmanuel continues to speak with Rehema, Jack and Diume. His mother occasionally sends them money to support themselves.

After one year . . . .

EMMAUEL: Sister!

RACHEL: Mmmm . . . I see you are really addicted to facebook!

EMMANUEL: Oh, I am really having fun here. Do you remember this lady who their family used to be our neighbour back in Uvira Congo?

RACHEL: Mmm, I don't remember. You know it has been such a long . . . .

EMMANUEL: Hold on . . . I show you her pictures . . . here she is . . .

RACHEL: Oh now I remember her. They live here in Canada. I had even forgotten to tell you about them. She is now a very beautiful lady as you can see from her photographs.

EMMANUEL: What do you think if I send her a friend request?

RACHEL: It is okay brother. Only take care please. Canada people are different from people back in Africa.

After 3 months

EMMANUEL:	Sister!!
RACHEL:	Yes . . .
EMMANUEL:	Merceline has send me her number . . . .
RACHEL:	Okay brother. Go slowly still. Here in Canada, women look for men not the other way round. Please don't get used to phone calls from women.
EMMANUEL:	Thank you sister for your timely advise all the time. You have good experience with people here in Canada. Do you think I should give her my number too or should I just call her if I love her.
RACHEL:	Good question Emmanuel. These girls from Canada are very intelligent and very cunning too. If you meet them the first time, tell them you like them. If you tell them you that you love them, they would rate you not serious at all. For Merceline, it is different. You need to ask her if she is dating someone here or not. If she says no, let her know that you have a friend here in Canada who saw her photos on facebook and see what she says about it.
EMMANUEL:	Oh my sister! What a brilliant idea!
RACHEL:	I know brother you are older than me and you are also wiser, but in life we all have to exchange ideas. I am not yet through, so if she asks you about your friend, now change the story and let her know it is you who wanted to be her friend.
EMMANUEL:	Mmm . . . . thank you little sister. You are full of wisdom! I love you!

Emmanuel calls Merceline

EMMANUEL: Hallo Merceline.

MERCELINE: Hallo Emmanuel. Long time.

EMMANUEL: Long time really . . . Only mountains don't meet. How is everyone?

MERCELINE: Everyone is okay here. How is your family?

EMMANUEL: We are all fine. Are you free now? I would like us to talk . . .

MERCELINE: Yes, Im free. We can talk . . .

EMMANUEL: If you don't mind, do you have a boyfriend?

MERCELINE: Why?

EMMANUEL: Oh . . . I have a friend who found me looking at your photographs on facebook. He was very excited and really liked your pictures . . . He asked me alot of questions that I had no answers so I decided to ask you . . . .

MERCELINE: Mmmm . . . okay. I am single for now. Does your friend know me from home or just saw me on facebook . . . .

EMMANUEL: I think he has loved you from facebook photos . . . .

MERCELINE: I see. I would like you to give him my number. How old is he, if I may ask?

EMMANUEL: Mmm . . . Merceline . . . . I think I like you. Let us not go far . . . What do you think?

MERCELINE: Mmmm . . . . Emmanuel, you really know how to set up traps! As I had told you I am is single for now and I am also looking for a partner. Today's world is more civilized. The African way of begging and waiting for a proposal is gone. I have no problem, we can be friends.

EMMANUEL: Im so grateful Merceline for letting me into your heart . . .

MERCELINE: Okay. Have no problem. I want to set the dining table for my mum. Let us talk later. Great time friend.

EMMANUEL: Okay. Thank you very much. bye

Next day . . . .

RACHEL: Brother, tell me now about Merceline . . . .

EMMANUEL: Sister, I am so grateful to you first for such brilliant ideas!! They worked! She is now mine . . . .

RACHEL: Congrats my brother. Now next thing, you need to buy lunch . . . .

EMMANUEL: Oh my sister. Im afraid, that is a good idea but I have no money . . .

RACHEL: Don't worry. Just call her, if she accepts we shall go for shopping then I can give you some money to entertain yourself . . . .

EMMANUEL: Thankyou very much sister. You are such a caring sister . . .

RACHEL: Don't worry brother. Fear results to poverty' and death. Im saying this because in life one has to be boldhearted and also have a no giving up attitude. All I can advise you is to avoid bad company here in Canada and whatever you want let me know. If she accepts to go out too with you let me know

EMMANUEL: Okay sister. I will let you know.

Emmanuel calls Merceline

EMMANUEL: Hallo Merceline

MERCELINE: Hallo Emmanuel. How are you?

EMMANUEL: I am very fine too. I need a favour please . . .

MERCELINE: Okay. Go ahead . . . .

EMMANUEL: Can I take you out for lunch please?

MARCELINE: Woooh . . . . Thats very nice. Let me know your plans . . . .

EMMANUEL: Can we have our lunch tommorrow?

MERCELINE: Okay. Let me know how we meet and where we go for lunch . . .

EMMANUEL: Okay let me check on my google earth then I can give you directions please . . . (*he reads out the street name and house number*)

MERCELINE: Okay . . . I see . . . But Emmanuel, I think I know around the city very well . . . . Let me come and will show you where to go . . .

EMMANUEL: Woh . . . I will wait for you then . . . .

MERCELINE: Okay babie . . . See you tommorrow . . . bye . . . love you . . .

EMMANUEL: I love you too . . .

RACHEL: Waoo . . . That is very good brother . . . .

EMMANUEL: Mmmm . . . sister . . . She has just called me babie . . . . Can't wait for the lunch tommorrow . . .

RACHEL: That's fine. Let's go for shopping. Are you taking a taxi tommorrow . . . . ?

EMMANUEL: She has said since she knows the city well, she will pick me up tommorrow. Let's go for shopping sister . . . .

RACHEL: That is very good if she will be here herself . . .

The following day

MERCELINE: Hallo Emmanuel . . .

EMMANUEL: Hello Merceline . . . . where are you . . .

MERCELINE: I'm right here infront of your house babie . . .

EMMANUEL: I am coming babie . . . One minute I will be there (*Emmanuel checks himself in the mirror and affirms to himself that he is handsome*)

Merceline is leaning outside her car. They happily exchange hugs

MERCELINE: Hi Babie Long time . . . .

EMMANUEL: Long time . . . I'm so excited to see you . . . .

MERCELINE: You look so smart . . . .

EMMANUEL: You look so beautiful my angel, I love your car too . . .

MERCELINE: Thank you Emmanuel, but a vehicle is normal here in Canada . . .

EMMANUEL: Yes, but still your vehicle model is very expensive too . . .

MERCELINE: True, It is expensive . . . .

EMMANUEL: You look gorgious babie . . . .

(They get into the car and they happily talk of their past back in Congo and their present lives)

MERCELINE: We have arrived. Have you been here before.?

EMMANUEL: No . . . I love the place! very quiet and relaxed atmosphere it is. You have a taste babie . . .

MERCELINE: Thanks babie . . .

EMMANUEL: I'm so grateful Merceline for giving me the chance in your life . . . .

MERCELINE: I am so grateful too for loving me . . . .

EMMANUEL: Thanks babie . . . . I think I have a problem when it comes to love . . . I love with all my heart. I hope we shall take care of our love to the end of our dreams . . .

MERCELINE: Oh . . . I see you fear getting hurt . . . .

EMMANUEL: Love belongs to two people. Naturally, a man loves a woman first and then the woman comes in, and the love is then shared through thin and thick . . . .

MERCELINE: You are right babie . . . .

EMMANUEL: So Merceline . . . let me know . . . what are your dreams.?

MERCELINE: My dream is to have a man who is humble and gentle. He should not be very rich neither poor. And you?

EMMANUEL: I always look for a gentle lady like you, a lady who loves a family and full of true love . . .

MERCELINE: I love your ideas, but I ask for one favour please babie . . .

EMMANUEL: Okay, go ahead . . .

MERCELINE: I ask if you can call me babie . . . .

EMMANUEL: okay, I love you babie . . .

They order for food as they share more about their dreams. They happily enjoy every moment as they eat. Finally they leave the restaurant, they part after spending time well . . .

EMMANUEL: Anybody home . . . . Im back home . . . . (*Emmanuel is joyfully whistling to himself*)

RACHEL: Welcome back . . . . I was actually thinking about you . . . mmm . . . How was it brother?

EMMANUEL: I have even come back with the money that you gave me . . . . here it is . . .

RACHEL: Wooow! I see she was loaded with money . . . What would you like to eat?

EMMANUEL: I am full sister . . . thanks . . .

RACHEL: Okay, I thought so too. Since it is late let us catch up in the morning. I'm so eager to hear the story of the day. Good night . . . .

EMMANUEL: Good night too . . . .

SCENE SIX

Emmanuel faces his past as a reality

RACHEL: Brother, Let us go for a walk . . . .

EMMANUEL: Okay . . . .

They arrive at a very relaxed park and they start a conversation

EMMANUEL: This park is very relaxed sister . . .

RACHEL: Yes, this is where people come for an evening walk . . .
            Let us sit over that bench (*they sit down*)

EMMANUEL: okay . . . .

RACHEL: I have something to tell you brother, I need your
            attention please . . . .

EMMANUEL: Okay sister, I am listening . . .

RACHEL: As you are now, you are in love with Merceline, do
            you want to marry her or you just want her for fun?

EMMANUEL: Oh . . . That is a very nice question . . . . I would love
            to marry her in the end . . . I am so madly in love
            with her for life!

RACHEL: Okay, that is really nice. If that is your plan that
            is very fine. All I ask is to let her know about your
            past.

EMMANUEL: Why?

RACHEL: You need to tell her you have a child with another
            woman. If you let her know you will have solved any

problems for your future. She will certainly trust you more.

EMMANUEL: I was also very hesitant about this issue because most ladies always dissappear immediately they know you have a child.

RACHEL: You are right. But a woman who loves you will love you with all your bargage.

EMMANUEL: That is very true sister. I will make sure she is aware of that.

At this point, Emmanuel opens up to Rachel about what he intents to do with the Rehema and her baby. After a while they walk back to the house.

The following day

EMMANUEL: Hallo babie . . . . How are you?

MERCELINE: Hallo babie . . . . I miss you . . . .

EMMANUEL: I wanted to know if tommorrow you are free. I want to buy you a cup of coffee. Is that okay with you babie?

MERCELINE: That's fine with me. Although I want us to go to another restaurant. I hope it is fine with you too . . .

EMMANUEL: Okay babie. Your choice is my best option . . . . see you tommorrow then . . .

MERCELINE: Okay babie . . . . bye

The next day Merceline and Emmanuel meet in another restaurant.

MERCELINE: Hi babie . . . .

EMMANUEL: Hi babie . . . . I have really missed you! Mmmm . . . babie . . . you really know very nice places. This place is wonderful . . .

MERCELINE: What do you prefer, we sit outside or inside . . . .

EMMANUEL: Anywhere babie . . . . though outside is better than inside since today is very hot. We need fresh air

MERCELINE: Okay, let sit over there (*they go to sit down*)

EMMANUEL: Okay babie . . . . Thank you for your love. I also love you very much. I believe we belong to each other. That is why I prefered we talk about our past so that we can be sure of ourselves . . .

MERCELINE: That's very good babie . . . . Can I start babie by telling you more about myself?

EMMANUEL: Yes babie . . . . you can start . . . .

MERCELINE: Really, I doubt if you know me very well since it is really a long time . . . . In short I am an orphan. I have never seen my father but my mum told me that my father passed away in a road accident. We moved to Canada before the civil war back in Congo together with my uncle Pascal. My mother and my uncle have supported me through my education and I thank God for both of them. My mother has been such a wonderful mother to me. I finished school one year ago and I am working now.

EMMANUEL: Im really sorry babie, I also lost my father too in the civil war, but I managed too see him. In my life, I have not stayed with my mother. I have survived very hard life alone. After the civil war, I had to survive from one refugee camp to another. I eventually found myself in Tanzania where I continued with my basic education. I found new friends, where I met a classmate by the name Rehema and it happened that I got her pregnant without my knowledge. I took the responsibility then, so I have a child . . . .

MERCELINE: Okay, I appreciate what I have just heard from you babie. I used to say that I cannot get married by a man with children, but one day I thought about it and came to a conclusion that I can get married by a man without children and I find no happiness at all so that would be absolute foolishness. Babie, I love you very much and I love you just as you are. That is very normal and by the time we loved each other alot had happened in our past.

EMMANUEL: Thank you babie . . . . for understanding my situation contrary to my expectation . . . . (*they hug each other*)

That episode ends. Soft music is played as they walk out of the restaurant slowly as they talk

Emmanuel at home

EMMANUEL: Sister you look tired . . . .

RACHEL: Yes brother I have been indoors working on the computer.

EMMANUEL: Canada life is abit boring since it is hard to visit neighours . . . By the way, this evening I was with Merceline and I have told her the truth about my past and she is very okay with everything . . .

RACHEL: I told you that she will be okay with it. All you needed was to tell her the truth. I bet she loves you even more!

EMMANUEL: Okay sister. Can we pay her a visit tommorrow in her house?

RACHEL: No problem. What time?

EMMANUEL: I think, tommorrow evening will be better.

The following day Emmanuel goes to visit Merceline together with his sister Rachel

MERCELINE: Oh . . . here you are babie . . . . I can see you are together with Rachel . . . Welcome . . .

RACHEL: Thank you. You are alone today?

MARCELINE: No, everybody is here. You know here in Canada, everybody stays indoor . . .

Merceline welcomes Emmanuel and his sister. After few minutes her mother and her uncle, Pascal joins them.

UNCLE PASCAL: Oooh . . . welcome . . .

EMMANUEL: Thank you uncle Pascal . . . .

UNCLE PASCAL: Feel at home . . .

MERCELINE: Mum . . . I am sure you remember Emmanuel very well. He is my boyfriend . . . Emmanuel, please meet my mother . . .

They greet each other

MERCELINE'S MOTHER: Oh . . . I am so happy for both of you. It is nice to also fall in love with a boy we know very well. But I have a question for you . . . As you know, Merceline is everything to me, she is my only child . . . Do you want to marry her?

EMMANUEL: Yes mum, I really want to marry your daughter. We are yet to plan the exact details.

MARCELINE'S MOTHER: That is very fine. Pascal, you have something to say . . .

UNCLE PASCAL: I am really happy for the two of you. It is good also they pray because they are all young and to also concentrate on their lives . . . Otherwise we wish you all the best. Yo are our children.

MERCELINE: We thank you for your blessings. Lets all go to the dining table. The food is ready . . .

UNCLE PASCAL: I request Rachel to pray.

(*Rachel prays for the food. They all eat together. After they finish eating Rachel will see Emmanel and his sister out*)

The following day

Emmanuel and Merceline have a converstion over the phone.

MERCELINE: Hallo babie, I am so grateful for the visit you paid to me yesterday. together with your sister. I love you so much sweetheart.

EMMANUEL: Okay babie. That is why I decided to come because I love you very much too. I think everything looks fine babie . . .

MERCELINE: I think it is high time we start thinking of our wedding . . .

EMMANUEL: Babie the only problem I have is lack of money. If I had money, I would marry you this year because I would have come to pay your dowry . . .

MERCELINE: Oh . . . I am very sorry. Just take heart all will be fine and patient. God will provide in good time.

EMMANUEL: Okay babie . . . Let's talk later. I love you.

MERCELINE: I love you too . . . bye

SCENE SEVEN

Date with destiny

After six months

EMMANUEL: Sister, since I started my job, I have been able to save alot. I think I have enough money to marry now . . .

RACHEL: Wooow! congratulations brother. If you are ready to marry, I am so ready to assist you in whichever way . . . All you need now is to ask Merceline if she is ready for marriage. If she is ready you can proceed and talk to her mother.

EMMANUEL: Okay sister. I will initiate the whole process from today.

RACHEL: And one more important thing brother, please make sure you don't talk over the phone. Go out with her and talk about it somewhere quiet. This is a very important agenda.

EMMANUEL: Thank you for that reminder . . .

The following day Merceline and Emmanuel meet in a restaurant

EMMANUEL: Babie . . . Im so grateful to God for enabling me to get a job. I have been able to save quite amount of money. I thought it wa wise we share this talk about something very important together.

All over sudden Emmanuel goes to his knees and removes a open box of a shinning wedding ring . . .

EMMANUEL: Will you marry me babie . . . .

Merceline looks around, everybody in the restaurant is cheering, feels abit shy but excited

She nods in acceptance as Emmanuel puts the angagement ring in her finger. He gets up then they continue talking.

MERCELINE: Woow! Im so happy. Babie . . . I am ready to get married by you and live with you forever . . .

EMMANUEL: Okay babie . . . I am so grateful for giving me the chance to be your husband. Marriage is not an easy task. We pray for patience and understanding in all circumstances partaining to life.

MERCELINE: I think you very well know I am the only child from my mother. I have no brother neither sister. You are my everything, so I will hold you with all my heart. I will never want to loose you.

EMMANUEL: Okay. I request you to let your mother know my mother will call her so that they can talk. Then you can also let me know what you mother thinks about the idea.

MERCELINE: Okay babie . . . I will let you know what they say.

They continue to talk as soft romantic soft music plays from the background. They leave after a while.

They part. Emmanuel at home.

EMMANUEL: Merceline has finally accepted my proposal! The next thing mum needs to talk to them so they arrange when to meet . . .

RACHEL: Good job brother. Let us wait to hear when Merceline's mother will be ready. We shall talk to mum once she is back.

EMMANUEL: Okay sister . . .

The same evening, Merceline holds a conversation with her mother and uncle Pascal . . .

MERCELINE: Mum and Uncle, I have something important to tell you before I leave for work.

UNCLE PASCAL: Okay. We are litening Merceline . . .

MERCELINE: I was able to talk to Emmanuel yesterday, and he said that he is ready to come and pay dowry at the end of this month. What do you say about that?

MERCLINE MOTHER: We have heard what you have said. Give us some time we talk about it, then we shall let you know about our decision.

UNCLE PASCAL: Okay my niece, since you want to become a mother there is no problem at all. I am ready to assist in any way as your father. Now give us some time we make a decision on that . . .

MERCELINE: One more thing is that Emanuel informed me that he has a child in Africa with another woman. I thought it was good I let you know. I am very grateful for everything. Let me leave you then by the time I come back i'm sure you will have made a decision.

MERCELINE'S MOTHER: Okay. See you later.

Merceline's mother seems to be in deep thoughts and hesitant about the whole issue of marriage. Uncle Pascal skeptic about it, drawa near to her . . .

UNCLE PASCAL: What are you thinking my sister?

MERCELINE'S MOTHER: I am very sure you remember how I gave birth to Merceline . . .

Immediately a flashback . . .

MERCELINE'S MOTHER: How are you Father?

PRIEST JEAN MARC: I am very fine. Had you come for the confession?

MERCELINE'S MOTHER: Yes . . .

PRIEST JEAN MARC: Okay, Welcome to the secret chambers. Please remove your shoes and wear a headscarf . . .

After the confession, the priest holds more intimate talk with Merceline's mother, then he foreces her to make love with him

MERCELINE'S MOTHER: You know I used to love you. Anyway, you did not use a condom . . . what if I become pregnant?

PRIEST JEAN MARC: If you become pregnant please take care of the baby. I will take care of everything. I love you. Keep that in mind

MERCELINES MOTHER: Okay, bye.

PRIEST JEAN MARC: Please have this money, It will assist you in future as today is my last day in Africa. I will be off to Italy for further studies. All I ask is keep this as a secret.

End of flash back

Abit of silence . . . .

MERCELINE'S MOTHER: That is how I got Merceline. I was a close friend of Emmanuel's mother so I am sure she knows all this very well . . .

UNCLE PASCAL: I think there is a big problem there since if Merceline will be married in that family she will eventually know the truth. I think it is better we deny her getting married to Emmanuel.

MERCELINE'S MOTHER: Oh, that is very fine brother. I had told her that her father had passed on and the truth is that he is still alive. I got out of Uvira and came to Canada and now it is coming back to me. I knew no one will ever tell her about it here . . .

UNCLE PASCAL: In this life, there is no secret that is hidden. The truth is, she will still know the truth if she gets married to Emmanuel. Although that was a great mistake you did, you could have told her the truth . . . it is her right to know the truth. She is now 23 years old and all this long she has always known that her father is dead.

MERCELINE'S MOTHER: What will be our reason then to deny her getting married to Emmanuel?

UNCLE PASCAL: We will have to deny her getting married to Pascal by the fact that he has achild with another woman.

MERCELINE'S MOTHER: That is a very brilliant idea!

After two weeks

MERCELINE: Now it is two weeks . . . I have not heard anything from you mother.

MERCELINE MOTHER: Okay, It has been a very hard decision to make but we have decided that you are not getting married to Emmanuel my dear . . .

MERCELINE: What is the reason if I may ask mum?

UNCLE PASCAL: The reason for this, is because Emmanuel has a child with another woman and we would not like you to get married to a man with another woman.

MERCELINE: Please listen to me carefully. Unless you have another reason that I am unaware, I am very comfortable with Emmanuel's baby. My happiness has nothing to do with the child but with Emmanuel whom I love very much . . .

MERCELINE'S MOTHER: We are final in that decision!!

MERCELINE: How comes you become so furious when I ask about this kind of decision. Remember I am 23 years old and if I get married now, I will spend the rest of my life with the man I love. If I get married, for better or worse it all depend on me. Whether you change your decision or not, it does not matter because I love Emmanuel and I cannot leave him. Legally I have all what it takes to marry him and the whole world will laugh at you only. (*she becomes very furious*)

UNCLE PASCAL: Get out of here!! As your uncle, I have spoken!!

Merceline rushes to her room frustrated and in tears. She talks to Emmanuel over the phone

MERCELINE: Babie . . . . I feel like dying . . . . !!!

EMMANUEL: Babie . . . . cool down and relax. Please tell me what is wrong . . . .

MERCELINE: Babie . . . my mother has said we cannot get married because you have a child already . . .

EMMANUEL: How comes and really I thought that concerned us. How comes it bothers them and it does not affect them at all . . .

MERCELINE: Babie . . . . I don't agree with them and I think I have a right to decide for myself what I want . . . .

EMMANUEL: Okay babie . . . let me talk to my mother and I am
              sure she will sort out this . . . . Relax and don't be
              troubled. I am sure we shall sort this out.

Emmanuel ends his conversation with Merceline

EMMANUEL: Mum . . . . !!! Rachel . . . . !!!
EMMANUEL'S MOTHER: Any problem Emmanuel?
RACHEL: What is wrong brother . . . .
EMMANUEL: Merceline has a problem. Her mother and her uncle
              don't want her to get married to me and this is really
              hurting her.
RACHEL: What could be the main reason for this?
EMMANUEL: The reason being I have a child already back in Africa.
EMMANUEL'S MOTHER: Mmmmmmmmmm . . . . My son listen
              carefully to me. I doubt if that is the main reason,
              there must be more than meets the eye. May be they
              are up to something else or they are trying to hide
              something. People change even after marriage. Be
              bold my son and take this very serious.
RACHEL: Im really sorry my brother but if God decide that she
              is your wife nothing can prevent that.

After one month . . .

UNCLE PASCAL: Sister, I am afraid that we have been unfair to
              Merceline. It is now one month and she is sad and
              peaceless. What do you think we do about it?

MARCELINE'S MOTHER: I think I have a solution. Since my daughter is so much in love with Emmanuel, I think It is better we do away with Emmanuel. Can you look for some thugs to kill him?

UNCLE PASCAL: That has been my idea for some time. I will certainly organise for that, but this must be between us only.

MERCELINE'S MOTHER: Here, get the cash and start work straight away . . .

UNCLE PASCAL: Okay . . . .

The following day, uncle Pascal manages to hire thugs. He organises and pays them ready to kill Emmanuel.

He then makes a phone call to Emmanuel

UNCLE PASCAL: Hallo Emmanuel. Uncle Merceline here . . . . How have you been?

EMMANUEL: Yes, I have heard your voice . . . .

UNCLE PASCAL: I believe Merceline had told you about our decision, I would like to meet you at the Park in the eveing we talk about this issue . . .

EMMANUEL: Okay . . . I will look into it . . .

That same day in the evening

UNCLE PASCAL: Emmanuel, we are men and there is a big problem and we need to sort it out amicably. The problem is Merceline has a father but her mother hid it from

her. Her father is alive and he lives in Italy. Priest Jean
Marc.

EMMANUEL: Mmmm . . . why did she have to do that? A catholic
priest?

UNCLE PASCAL: And due to that let me leave. I am not feeling
well . . . .

EMMANUEL: I doubt that we are done with talking . . . . Uncle
Pascal, what are you up to?

UNCLE PASCAL: Hey guys!!! do your work . . .

EMMANUEL: Oh God . . . . Have mercy on me . . . Help somebody

Emmanuel is beaten mercilessly and left for the dead

At midnight

RACHEL: How comes Emmanuel is not yet back and it is now
midnight?

EMMANUEL'S MOTHER: I was just about to ask you that. It is always his
culture to be back by 8 pm. May be he has gone to see
Merceline but if it gets to 2 a.m please call the police . . .

RACHEL: Yes, his number is not going through . . . Let me call
Merceline . . . .

EMMANUEL'S MOTHER: Yes please . . . .

Rachel makes a phone call to Merceline

RACHEL: Hello Merceline . . . Rachel here . . . .

MERCELINE: Yes. How was your day?

RACHEL: Fine, thank you. We wanted to know if you had seen Emmanuel . . . It is now almost 6 a.m and he has not yet arrrived . . . .

MERCELINE: No . . . . He has not called me . . . I have also been trying his number and it is not going through. I think we try to call the police . . .

RACHEL: Okay. Let me do that straight away. bye

EMMANUEL MOTHER: What did she say?

RACHEL: She has also been looking for him . . . . Lets call the police mum . . .

EMMANUEL'S MOTHER: Okay . . . lets call the police . . .

Rachel calls the police line

EMMANUEL'S MOTHER: What is police saying?

RACHEL: They have no report whatsoever. They will make a call to me immediately they have a report . . .

Rachel receives a phone call from Merceline

MERCELINE: Hallo Rachel . . . . Any report?

RACHEL: No Merceline, though we have rported to the police and they have said immediately they get any information they will call us . . . .

MERCELINE: Okay . . . I will also invetigate . . .

After three hour Rachel receives a phone call from the police

RACHEL: Yes . . . Who I'm I speaking to please?

POLICE: I am calling from police station. We have managed
            to get the body of your brother . . . He is not dead.
            We have been able to identify him by documents that
            were in his pocket that had the names that you gave
            us. We have taken him to the hospital. He is in third
            floor Canada Hospital. He has managed to talk and
            has said he wants to talk to a lady called Merceline
            immediately. Do you know her?

RACHEL: Yes I do. It is his fiancee. Thank you very much, We
            shall surely be there as soon as possible.

Rachel immediately tells her mother what has just ensued. She then makes
a phone call to Merceline

RACHEL: Hallo Merceline . . . The police have just called us
            and told us that they found Emmanuel's body and he
            is now in hospital. We are heading there. Emmanuel
            wants to talk to you immediately please. If it is
            possible let us meet there.

MERCELINE: Oh my God!!! My dear Emmanuel . . . . Okay . . . Let
            me tell mum and uncle . . . Let me know if there is
            any more information. I will be there as soon as I can.

RACHEL: We are heading there right now . . . . bye

MERCELINE: Okay . . . bye

MERCELINE: What is wrong dear?

MERCELINE: Mum . . . Emmanuel is in hospital in really a bad condition . . . .

UNCLE PASCAL: What happened?

EMMANUEL'S MOTHER: The police have been able to collect his body in bad condition and have taken him to hospital . . .

UNCLE PASCAL: Has he died . . . ?

MERCELINE: No, he is alive . . . . he is in a bad condition . . . I need to see him now . . . .

MERCELINE'S MOTHER: Why should we take you? You can do it alone. I told you that I don't want to hear anything about Emmanuel in this house! Your uncle and I are not leaving here. We have frequently told you that it could be possible that Emmanuel is a thug. How comes that he was found beaten without a reason?

UNCLE PASCAL: Yes, we are not leaving here. Just look for means by yourself.

MERCELINE (*she gets very furious*) Listen to me carefully! I really don't understand how heartless you have become. I doubt if you are really my relatives. I'm ready to die for the sake of Emmanuel. Take it or leave it.

MERCELINE MOTHER: Now you understand. We are not your relatives . . . Me and your uncle we are born of the same mother. Do you really have a brother or sister here?

MERCELINE: I am tired of both of you. I have endured enough. (*she snatches a gun from her bag*) Will you go or not?

MERCELINE MOTHER: Pascal let us go now . . . . Please put the gun down . . .

UNCLE PASCAL: Okay, lets go. Put your gun down . . .

Merceline's mother and ncle pascal gets up and heads to the car shaking

MERCELINE: No more talk!! Right now!!

Rachel calls Merceline and informs her where exactly Emmanuel is hospitalized.

MERCELINE: Okay Rachel (*Rachel orders her uncle to drive the vehicle and they leave . . .*

At the hospital

RACHEL: What happened brother?

EMMANUEL: I would have died today and Im sure you wouldhave missed me . . .

EMMANUEL'S MOTHER: Wa happened my son?

Merceline enters with her uncle and mother

EMMANUEL: I can see you are here now to finish me. Merceline please get away. All I did was to love you. If I wronged you please forgive me.

RACHEL: Emmanuel, this is your fiancee? What is not happening?

EMMANUEL: Life has never been fair. The devil is always like a roaring lion looking for someone to devour. Merceline my love trust no one in this world.

EMMANUEL'S MOTHER: What is not happening here . . . Can someone tell me . . .

EMMANUEL: Mum, yesterday, Pascal gave me a call and told me that he wanted us to talk about Merceline and our marriage issue. Merceline, believe it or not, your mother is a murderer. Your uncle told me the truth about your father and after that he had hired thugs who beat me almost to death. Their only solution for you was to see me dead since I knew their secret that she has hidden from you all these years. But there are no secrets in life, just hidden truths that lie beneath the surface.

MERCELINE: Is that true mum and uncle?

MERCELINE MOTHER: (trembling) Yes, your father is alive and he is in italy. Priest Jean Marc. Becaue of disgrace, I had to hide it to from the society. Emmanuel's mother was my friend from childhood. She knows everything and the whole truth. We only feared you getting married in this family my dear and definately you will come to know one day. We opted to kill Emmanuel . . .

MERCELINE: Now I really don't need that father because I am big now . . . I also really don't need both of you. Now that you wanted to kill my Emmanuel I will kill you. Say your last prayers.

EMMANUEL: Babie . . . don't do that . . . .

MERCELINE: No . . . . don't come near me . . . . I don't need them any more . . .

EMMANUEL: Don't . . . .

Finally Rachel and Emmanuel manages to get the gun out of Merceline's hands.

The two families reconciles and Merceline forgives her mother and her uncle. She finally gets married to Emmanuel.

All these time, Rehema's baby was finally confirmed that Emmanuel was not the father through a DNA test. Jack and Diume also went back to school to study.

- - - *End* - - -

FILM CAST

- EMMANUEL
- REHEMA
- TEACHER
- JACK
- DIEUME
- PATRICK
- REHEMA'S BABY
- RACHEL
- EMMANUEL'S MOTHER
- MARCELINE
- PATRICK

- UNCLE PASCAL
- MARCELINE MOTHER:
- JAMES
- DOCTOR
- 3 THUGS WHO ATTACK EMMANUEL
- POLICE

VENUE OF CAST

- VILLAGE
- FARM AND VILLAGE HOUSE
- EMMANUEL'S HOUSE
- MERCELINE'S HOUSE
- PARK
- HOSPITAL
- GOOD HOTELS
- BUFFET PLACE
- SHOPPING MALL

EQUIPMENT FOR CAST

- 2 VEHICLES
- MOBILE PHONE
- AIRPORT IN AFRICA

www.ingramcontent.com/pod-product-compliance
Lightning Source LLC
Chambersburg PA
CBHW021017180526
45163CB00005B/1996